KU-337-926

Clothes long ago

Elizabeth Paren and Gill Stacey

Oxford University Press

Mrs Scott found some old clothes.

Her family wore them long ago.

She told the children about the clothes.

Contents

Clothes for every day

gymslip

strap
shoes

When I was a child I wore a
uniform to school.
I wore a gymslip and strap shoes.

School coats and hats

overall

Mum washed our clothes in the sink.

She wore an overall.

This kept her own clothes dry.

Clothes for work

protective clothes

Dad worked on the trains.

The work was hot and dirty.

He wore special clothes to protect him.

Mum was a waitress in a cafe.

She had to look smart.

She wore a cap to keep her hair tidy.

Clothes for play

knitted swimming
costume

Sometimes we went to the seaside.

I wore a knitted swimming costume.

It went baggy when it got wet.

Boys always wore short trousers.

Dad liked to play football.

Mum made him a pair of shorts.

She cut the legs off his old trousers.

Making clothes

We did not buy many clothes from shops.

Mum made all my dresses at home.

One day she made me a special dress.

Patterns for making clothes

sewing machine

material

pattern

She bought a pattern and some material.

She cut out the material.

She sewed it on the sewing machine.

Buying clothes

Everyone wore hats.

We saved up to buy new clothes.
Sometimes, Mum bought a new hat.

12

tailor

Once, Dad needed a new suit.

He went to the tailor.

The tailor measured him and

then made the suit.

Clothes for a special day

We all dressed up on the day of
Princess Elizabeth's wedding.
The women put on their best dresses.
They wore hats and gloves too.

The royal wedding

My new dress had a lace collar and puffed sleeves.

Index

Oxford University Press,
Great Clarendon Street,
Oxford OX2 6DP

© Oxford University Press
All rights reserved

First published by Oxford University
Press 1997

ISBN 0 19 916932 2

Available in packs
Clothes Pack (one of each title)
ISBN 0 19 916934 9
Clothes Class Pack (six of each title)
ISBN 0 19 916935 7

Acknowledgements

Illustrated by: Alex Brychta (p2) and
Chris Molan.

The Publisher would like to thank the
following for permission to reproduce
photographs: Barnaby's Picture Library
(p7); Hulton Deutsch Collection Ltd
(pp9, 12, 15); News Team International/
Oxford Times (p5).
All other photographs were taken by
Martin Sookias.

Cover illustration: Chris Molan.

Cover photo: Michael Dudley.

Printed and bound in Hong Kong